AITAREYA UPANISHAD.
De-gendering Hinduism.

SERIES EDITOR: TAPATI BHARADWAJ.

Published by

LIES AND BIG FEET

ISBN: 8192875296
ISBN-13: 978-8192875293

PREFATORY NOTE:

This rendition of an Upanishadic text is but a part of a larger series; the aim of this work is to construe Hindu religious texts as literature, and examine them within a gendered inflected analytical framework. What prevents us from examining the Upanishadic or the Vedic texts within a literary or a gendered perspective? If the basis of religion is "revealed knowledge," which was made evident to men – then is it not obvious that these notions of the Absolute Being would but be defined within gender inflected terminologies? The personal gender-biases of men would affect and predetermine how the notions of the Supreme Being were written about.

Let me explain with an example from an Upanishad. In the Aitareya Upanishad, the first stanza reads in the following manner:

"Om! In the beginning this was but the Absolute Self alone. There was nothing else whatsoever that winked. It thought, 'Let Me create the world.'"

We have to keep in mind that the Vedic texts are partially truthful – they are correct in their explanations on the notion of Absolute Consciousness which becomes matter, and there is no gender ascribed to this Absolute Being. The "Absolute Self" is denoted within gender neutral terms and is referred to as "It."

But there is a slippage which occurs in the Vedic texts, making these texts suspect: it reveals the fact that those who were writing about this kind of revealed, divine knowledge were men and their interests are evident in how the notion of Absolute Consciousness is defined and described. In the same Vedic text, we will find gender specific characteristics of the Absolute Being. The second stanza of the Aitreya Upanishad reads in the following manner:

"He created these worlds, viz. *ambhas, marici, mara* and *apah*. That which is beyond heaven is *ambhas*. Heaven is its support. The sky is *marici*. The earth is *mara*. The worlds that are below are the *apah*."

A shift occurs whereby, "It" becomes "He": and we all assume, and accept, that the Absolute Being has to be male.

To follow this statement to its conclusion, we can state that as the Vedic texts equate the "Absolute Self" with the masculine, men are seen as being agents; in the second part of the <u>Aitreya Upanishad</u>, the first stanza reads: "In man indeed is the soul first conceived"; the implication is that men are agents in determining the birth of children while women are mere passive receptacles.

Biological sciences make use of these dichotomies, and feminists have critiqued how biology (which should be an objective science) makes use of the dominant trope of the "passive" female egg and the "active" male sperm. It is a notion that has also been used since times immemorial in the western worlds, beginning with Aristotle and St. Thomas.

There is no attempt by any religious institution to undress these entrenched misogyny that exists in Hinduism; and these dominant mainstream institutions simply reiterate the status quo. If we pick up a random text on religion that has been published by a well-recognized, religious institution, like the Ramakrishna Mission (that is seen as epitomising modern Hinduism), we find a similar trope operating as the subtext.

In <u>How is a man Reborn</u>, a short text that was published in 1970, by Advaita Ashrama, the publishing house of the Ramakrishna Mission, Swami Satprakashananda makes use of the same above mentioned dichotomy (pp.43-48); he cites instances from the <u>Chandogya Upanishad</u>, the <u>Brhadaranyaka Upanishad</u>, one Dr. Sturtevant, the <u>Aitareya</u>

<u>Upanishad</u> and Sankara to prove the same point, whereby women are seen as passive agents whose only role in society is to procreate while men and sons do all the active work.

We can but make a beginning in dismantling these texts on Hinduism by re-transcribing them. The hope is that our daughters will be able to live in a gender –neutral society.

<u>THE ARRANGEMENT OF THE TEXT:</u>

ON THE LEFT SIDE, THERE IS THE OLDER VERSION OF THE AITERAYA UPANISHAD AND THE RIGHT SIDE HAS A REVISED VERSION OF THE TEXT.

AITAREYA UPANISHAD

PART I.

Chapter 1.

1. *Om*! In the beginning this was but the absolute Self alone. There was nothing else whatsoever that winked. It thought, 'Let Me create the worlds.'

1. *Om*! In the beginning this was but the absolute Self alone. There was nothing else whatsoever that winked. It thought, 'Let Me create the worlds.'

2. He created these worlds, viz. *ambhas, maríci, mara, ápah.* That which is beyond heaven is *ambhas.* Heaven is its support. The sky is *maríci.* The earth is *mara.* The worlds that are below are the *ápah.*

2. S/he/ It created these worlds, viz. *ambhas, maríci, mara, ápah*. That which is beyond heaven is *ambhas*. Heaven is its support. The sky is *maríci*. The earth is *mara*. The worlds that are below are the *ápah*.

3. He thought, 'These then are
   the worlds. Let Me create
   the protectors of the worlds.'
   Having gathered up a (lump
   of the) human form from the
   water itself, He gave shape
   to it.

3. S/he/It thought, 'These then are the worlds. Let Me create the protectors of the worlds.' Having gathered up a (lump of the) human form from the water itself, S/he/It gave shape to it.

4.   He deliberated with regard to Him (i.e. Virát of the human form). As He (i.e. Virát) was being deliberated on, His (i.e. Varát's) mouth parted, just as an egg does. From the mouth emerged speech; from speech came Fire. The nostrils parted; from the nostrils came out the sense of smell; from the sense of smell came Váyu (Air). The two eyes parted; from the eyes emerged the sense of sight; from the sense of sight came the Sun. The two ears parted; from the ears came the sense of hearing; from the sense of hearing came the Directions. The skin emerged; from the skin came out hair (i.e. the sense of touch associated with hair); from the sense of touch came the Herbs and Trees. The heart took shape; from the heart issued the internal organ (mind); from the internal organ came the Moon. The navel parted; from the navel came out the organ of ejection; from the organ of ejection issued Death. The seat of the procreative organ parted; from that came the procreative organ; from the procreative organ came out Water.

4.   S/he deliberated with regard to Her/Him/ It (i.e. Virát of the human form). As S/he/It (i.e. Virát) was being deliberated on, Her/His/It's (i.e. Varát's) mouth parted, just as an egg does. From the mouth emerged speech; from speech came Fire. The nostrils parted; from the nostrils came out the sense of smell; from the sense of smell came Váyu (Air). The two eyes parted; from the eyes emerged the sense of sight; from the sense of sight came the Sun. The two ears parted; from the ears came the sense of hearing; from the sense of hearing came the Directions. The skin emerged; from the skin came out hair (i.e. the sense of touch associated with hair); from the sense of touch came the Herbs and Trees. The heart took shape; from the heart issued the internal organ (mind); from the internal organ came the Moon. The navel parted; from the navel came out the organ of ejection; from the organ of ejection issued Death. The seat of the procreative organ parted; from that came the procreative organ; from the procreative organ came out Water.

CHAPTER II.

1. These deities, that had been created, fell into this vast ocean. He subjected Him (i.e. Virát) to hunger and thirst. They said to Him (i.e. to the Creator), 'Provide an abode for us, staying where we can eat food.'

1. These deities, that had been created, fell into this vast ocean. S/he/It subjected Her/Him (i.e. Virát) to hunger and thirst. They said to Her/Him/It (i.e. to the Creator), 'Provide an abode for us, staying where we can eat food.'

2. For them He (i.e. God) brought a cow. They said, 'This one is certainly not adequate for us.' For them He brought a horse. They said, 'This one is certainly not adequate for us.'

2. For them S/he/It (i.e. God) brought a cow. They said, 'This one is certainly not adequate for us.' For them S/he/It brought a horse. They said, 'This one is certainly not adequate for us.'

3. For them He brought a man. They said, 'This one is well formed; man indeed is a creation of God Himself.' To them He said, 'Enter into your respective abodes.'

3. For them S/he/It brought a man. They said, 'This one is well formed; man indeed is a creation of God Herself/Himself/ It.' To them S/he/It said, 'Enter into your respective abodes.'

4. Fire entered into the mouth taking the form of the organ of speech. Air entered into the nostrils assuming the form of the sense of smell; the Sun entered into the eyes as the sense of sight; the Directions entered into the ears by becoming the sense of hearing; the Herbs and Trees entered into the skin in the form of hair (i.e. the sense of touch); the Moon entered into the heart in the shape of the mind; Death entered into the navel in the form of Apána (i.e. the vital force that presses down); Water entered into the limb of generation in the form of semen (i.e. the organ of procreation).

4. Fire entered into the mouth taking the form of the organ of speech. Air entered into the nostrils assuming the form of the sense of smell; the Sun entered into the eyes as the sense of sight; the Directions entered into the ears by becoming the sense of hearing; the Herbs and Trees entered into the skin in the form of hair (i.e. the sense of touch); the Moon entered into the heart in the shape of the mind; Death entered into the navel in the form of Apána (i.e. the vital force that presses down); Water entered into the limb of generation in the form of ovum/semen (i.e. the organ of procreation).

5. To Him Hunger and Thirst said, 'Provide for us (some abode).' To them He said 'I provide your livelihood among these very gods; I make you share in their portions.' Therefore when oblation is taken up (for being offered) for any deity whichsoever, Hunger and Thirst become verily sharers with that deity.

5. To Her/Him/It Hunger and Thirst said, 'Provide for us (some abode).' To them S/he/It said 'I provide your livelihood among these very Divine Beings; I make you share in their portions.' Therefore when oblation is taken up (for being offered) for any deity whichsoever, Hunger and Thirst become verily sharers with that deity.

CHAPTER III.

1. He thought, 'This, then, are the senses and the deities of the senses. Let me create food for them.'

1. S/he/It thought, 'This, then, are the senses and the deities of the senses. Let me create food for them.'

2. He deliberated with regard to the water. From the water, thus brooded over, evolved a form. The form that emerged was verily food.

2. S/he/It deliberated with
   regard to the water. From
   the water, thus brooded
   over, evolved a form. The
   form that emerged was verily
   food.

3. This food, that was created, turned back and attempted to run away. He tried to take it up with speech. He did not succeed in taking it up through speech. If He had succeeded in taking it up with the speech, then one would have become contented merely by talking of food.

3. This food, that was created, turned back and attempted to run away. S/he/It tried to take it up with speech. S/he-It did not succeed in taking it up through speech. If S/he/It had succeeded in taking it up with the speech, then one would have become contented merely by talking of food.

4. He tried to grasp that food with the sense of smell. He did not succeed in grasping it by smelling. If He had succeeded in grasping it by smelling, then, everyone would have become contented merely by smelling food.

4. S/he/It tried to grasp that food with the sense of smell. S/he/It did not succeed in grasping it by smelling. If S/he/It had succeeded in grasping it by smelling, then, everyone would have become contented merely by smelling food.

5. He wanted to take up the food with the eye. He did not succeed in taking it up with the eye. If He had taken it up with the eye, then everyone would have become satisfied by merely seeing food.

5. S/he/It wanted to take up the food with the eye. S/he/It did not succeed in taking it up with the eye. If S/he/It had taken it up with the eye, then everyone would have become satisfied by merely seeing food.

6. He wanted to take up the food with the ear. He did not succeed in taking it up with the ear. If He had taken it up with the ear, then everyone would have become satisfied merely by hearing of food.

6. S/he wanted to take up the food with the ear. S/he did not succeed in taking it up with the ear. If S/he had taken it up with the ear, then everyone would have become satisfied merely by hearing of food.

7. He wanted to take it up with
   the sense of touch. He did
   not succeed in taking it up
   with the sense of touch. If
   He had taken it up with
   touch, then everyone would
   have been satisfied merely
   be touching food.

7. S/he wanted to take it up with the sense of touch. S/he did not succeed in taking it up with the sense of touch. If S/he had taken it up with touch, then everyone would have been satisfied merely be touching food.

8. He wanted to take it up with the mind. He did not succeed in taking it up with the mind. If He had taken it up with the mind, then everyone would have become satisfied by merely thinking of food.

8.   S/he wanted to take it up with the mind. S/he did not succeed in taking it up with the mind. If S/he had taken it up with the mind, then everyone would have become satisfied by merely thinking of food.

9. He wanted to take it up with the procreative organ. He did not succeed in taking it up with the procreative organ. If He had taken it up with the procreative organ, then everyone would have become satisfied by merely ejecting food.

9. S/he wanted to take it up with the procreative organ. S/he did not succeed in taking it up with the procreative organ. If S/he had taken it up with the procreative organ, then everyone would have become satisfied by merely ejecting food.

10. He wanted to take it up with Apána. He took it up. This is the devourer of food. That vital energy which is well known as dependant on food for its subsistence is this vital energy (called Apána).

10. S/he wanted to take it up with Apána. S/he took it up. This is the devourer of food. That vital energy which is well known as dependant on food for its subsistence is this vital energy (called Apána).

11. He thought, 'How indeed can it be there without Me?' He thought, 'Through which of the two ways should I enter?' He thought, 'If utterance is done by the organ of speech, smelling by the sense of smell, seeing by the eye, hearing by the ear, feeling by the sense of touch, thinking by the mind, the act of drawing in (or pressing down) by Apána, ejecting by the procreative organ, then who (or what) am I?'

11. S/he thought, 'How indeed can it be there without Me?' S/he thought, 'Through which of the two ways should I enter?' S/he thought, 'If utterance is done by the organ of speech, smelling by the sense of smell, seeing by the eye, hearing by the ear, feeling by the sense of touch, thinking by the mind, the act of drawing in (or pressing down) by Apána, ejecting by the procreative organ, then who (or what) am I?'

12. Having split up this very
    end, He entered through this
    door. This entrance is
    known as *vidrti* (the cleft
    entrance). Hence, it is
    delightful. Of Him there are
    three abodes – three (states
    of) dream. This one is an
    abode, this one is an abode,
    this one is an abode.

12. Having split up this very end, S/he entered through this door. This entrance is known as *vidrti* (the cleft entrance). Hence, it is delightful. Of Her/Him there are three abodes – three (states of) dream. This one is an abode, this one is an abode, this one is an abode.

13. Being born, He manifested all the beings; for did He speak of (or know) anything else? He realised this very Purusa as Brahman, the most pervasive, thus: 'O! I have realised this.'

13. Being born, S/he manifested all the beings; for did S/he speak of (or know) anything else? S/he realised this very Purusa as Brahman, the most pervasive, thus: 'O! I have realised this.'

14. Therefore His name is Idandra. He is verily known as Idandra. Although He is Idandra, they call Him indirectly Indra; for the gods are verily fond of indirect names, the gods are verily fond of indirect names.

14. Therefore Her/His/Its name is Idandra. S/he/It is verily known as Idandra. Although S/he/It is Idandra, they call Her/Him/It indirectly Indra; for the gods are verily fond of indirect names, the gods are verily fond of indirect names.

PART II.
CHAPTER I.

1. In man indeed is the soul first conceived. That which is this semen is extracted from all the limbs as their vigour. He holds that self of his in his own self. When he sheds it into his wife, then he procreates it. That is its first birth.

1. In wo/man indeed is the soul first conceived. That which is this ovum/semen is extracted from all the limbs as their vigour. S/he holds that self of hers/him in her/his own self. When s/he receives/sheds it into her/his partner, then s/he procreates it. That is its first birth.

2. That becomes non-different from the wife, just as much as her own limb is. Therefore (the foetus) does not hurt her. She nourishes this self of his that has entered here (in her womb).

2. That becomes non-different from the parent, just as much as the parent's own limb is. Therefore (the foetus) does not hurt the person carrying it. She nourishes this self of the parents that has entered here (in her womb).

3. She, the nourisher, becomes fit to be nourished [protected]. The wife bears that embryo (before the birth). He (the father) protects the son at the very start, soon after his birth. That he protects the son at the very beginning, just after birth, thereby he protects his own self for the sake of the continuance of these worlds. For thus is the continuance of these world ensured. That is his second birth.

3. She, the nourisher, becomes fit to be nourished [protected]. The wife bears that embryo (before the birth). The parents protects the child at the very start, soon after its birth. That the parent protects the child at the very beginning, just after birth, thereby the parent protects its own self for the sake of the continuance of these worlds. For thus is the continuance of these world ensured. That is the parent's second birth.

4. This self of his (viz. the son) is deputed (by the father) for the performance of virtuous deeds. Then this other self of his (that is the father of the son), having got his duties fulfilled and having advanced in age, departs. As soon as he departs, he takes birth again. That is his third birth.

4. This self of the parent (viz. the child) is deputed (by the parent) for the performance of virtuous deeds. Then this other self of the child (that is the parent of the child), having got its duties fulfilled and having advanced in age, departs. As soon as s/he departs, s/he takes birth again. That is the parent's third birth.

5. This fact was stated by the seer: 'Even while lying in the womb, I came to know of the birth of all the gods. A hundred iron citadels held me down. Then, like a hawk, I forced my way through by dint of the knowledge of the Self.' Vámadeva said this while still lying in the mother's womb.

5. This fact was stated by the wise one: 'Even while lying in the womb, I came to know of the birth of all the Divine Beings. A hundred iron citadels held me down. Then, like a hawk, I forced my way through by dint of the knowledge of the Self.' Vámadevi/deva said this while still lying in the mother's womb.

6. He who had known thus (had) become identified with the Supreme, and attained all desirable things (even here); and having (then) ascended higher up after the destruction of the body, he became immortal, in the world of the Self. He became immortal.

6. S/he who had known thus
    (had) become identified with
    the Supreme, and attained
    all desirable things (even
    here); and having (then)
    ascended higher up after the
    destruction of the body,
    s/he became immortal, in
    the world of the Self. S/he
    became immortal.

PART III.

CHAPTER I.

1. *Om*! Which is It that we worship as this Self? Which of the two is the Self? Is It that by which one sees, and by which one hears; also, by which one smells odour, and by which one utters speech, and by which one tastes the sweet or the sour?

1. *Om*! Which is It that we worship as this Self? Which of the two is the Self? Is It that by which one sees, and by which one hears; also, by which one smells odour, and by which one utters speech, and by which one tastes the sweet or the sour?

2. It is this heart (intellect) and this mind that were stated earlier. It is sentience, rulership, secular knowledge, presence of mind, retentiveness, sense-perception, fortitude, thinking, genius, mental suffering, memory, ascertainment, resolution, life-activities, hankering, passion, and such others. All these verily are the names of Consciousness.

2. It is this heart (intellect) and this mind that were stated earlier. It is sentience, rulership, secular knowledge, presence of mind, retentiveness, sense-perception, fortitude, thinking, genius, mental suffering, memory, ascertainment, resolution, life-activities, hankering, passion, and such others. All these verily are the names of Consciousness.

3. This One is (the inferior) Brahman;
    this is Indra, this is Prajápati; this
    is all these gods; and this is these
    five elements, viz. earth, air, space,
    water, fire; and this is all these (big
    creatures), together with the tiny
    ones, that are the procreators of
    others and referable in pairs – to
    wit, those that are born of eggs, of
    wombs, of moisture, and of the
    earth, viz. horses, cattle, men,
    elephants, and all the creatures that
    there are which move or fly and
    those which do not move. All these
    are impelled by Consciousness; all
    these have Consciousness as the
    giver of their reality; the universe
    has Consciousness as its eye, and
    Consciousness is it end.
    Consciousness is Brahman.

3. This One is (the inferior) Brahman;
    this is Indra, this is Prajápati; this
    is all these Divine Beings; and this
    is these five elements, viz. earth,
    air, space, water, fire; and this is all
    these (big creatures), together with
    the tiny ones, that are the
    procreators of others and referable
    in pairs – to wit, those that are born
    of eggs, of wombs, of moisture,
    and of the earth, viz. horses, cattle,
    men, elephants, and all the
    creatures that there are which
    move or fly and those which do not
    move. All these are impelled by
    Consciousness; all these have
    Consciousness as the giver of their
    reality; the universe has
    Consciousness as its eye, and
    Consciousness is it end.
    Consciousness is Brahman.

4. Through this Self that is Consciousness, he ascended higher up from this world, and getting all desires fulfilled in that heavenly world, he became immortal, he became immortal.

4. Through this Self that is Consciousness, s/he ascended higher up from this world, and getting all desires fulfilled in that heavenly world, s/he became immortal, s/he became immortal.

ABOUT THE AUTHOR

I grew up in an uber-brahmanical family where ritualistic worship was a part of my everyday life; the Vedic texts and the Upanishads were also something I grew up. I always thought that religion was something "out" there; I never actually thought that we were meant to believe in these texts on "revealed knowledge" in an absolute manner. But religion pervades every and all aspects of our lives – institutional, private or public, and be they secular, or not.

After reading the Hindu religious texts for myself, I realised how gendered these texts were, and to our sensibilities, the archaic notions that underlie the basic tenets of Hinduism sound ridiculous and perverse. We forget that the "revealed knowledge" that is evident in the Upanishads has been written by men, and their gender predetermined how they translated the notions of the Absolute Being into language.

I do not want my daughter to grow up within such a flawed belief system; we have to dismantle the existing religious texts as they are and re-transcribe them in order to arrive at gender-neutral concepts of religion, and Being.

www.ingramcontent.com/pod-product-compliance
Lightning Source LLC
Chambersburg PA
CBHW060658030426
42337CB00017B/2676